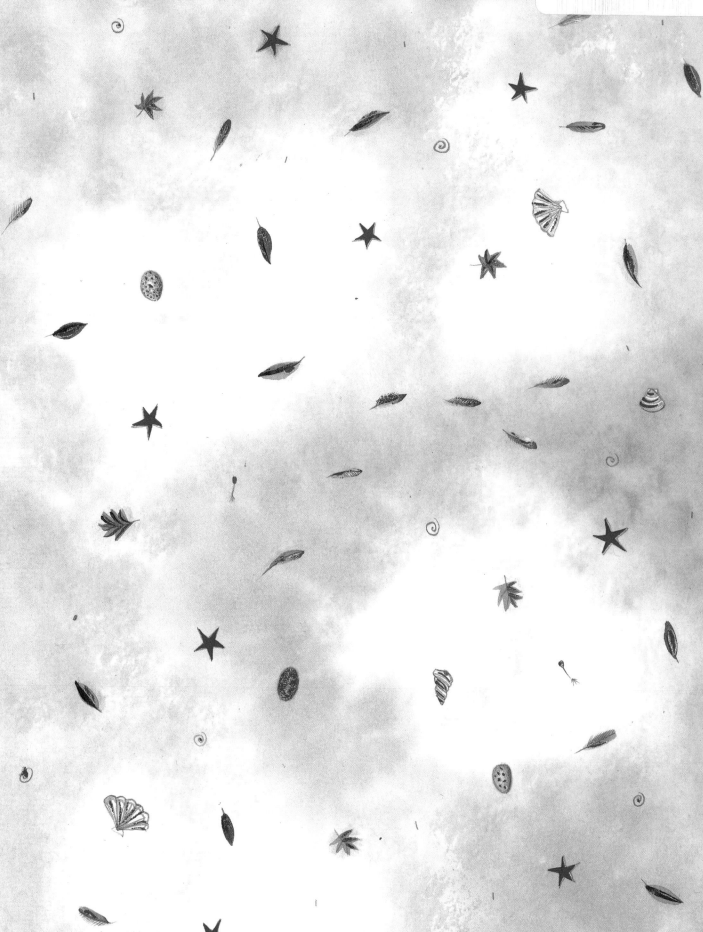

·In·the·
·Beginning·

For Ian, Margot, Eleanor, John and Sophie Lawrence
with love
J.R.

ORCHARD BOOKS
96 Leonard Street
London EC2A 4RH
Orchard Books Australia
14 Mars Road Lane Cove, NSW 2066
ISBN 1 86039 456 6
This edition first published in Great Britain in 1997
© Jane Ray 1990, 1991, 1992
The right of Jane Ray to be identified as illustrator of this work
has been asserted by them in accordance with the Copyright, Designs and Patents Act, 1988.
A CIP catalogue record for this book is available from the British Library.
Printed in Singapore

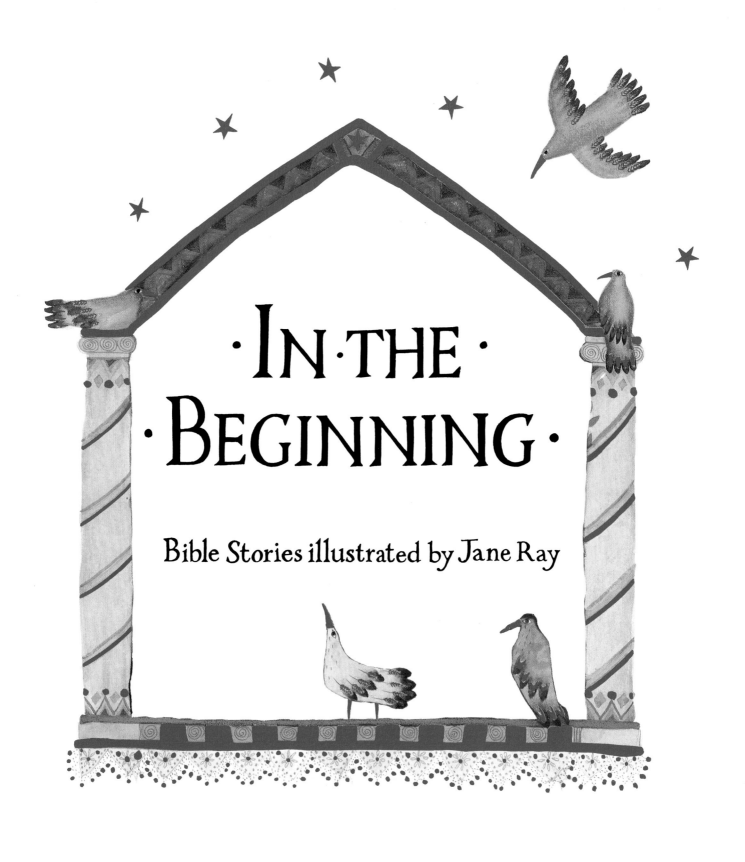

·In·the·
·Beginning·

Bible Stories illustrated by Jane Ray

ORCHARD BOOKS

.THE·STORY·OF. .THE·CREATION.

This is how the world began.

In the beginning deep waters covered the earth,
and it was empty and dark, without any shape.
And God saw there was work for him to do.

God said, "Let there be light!" and there was light.
And God divided the light from the darkness.
He called the light day and the darkness he called night.
And the evening and the morning were the first day.

day

night

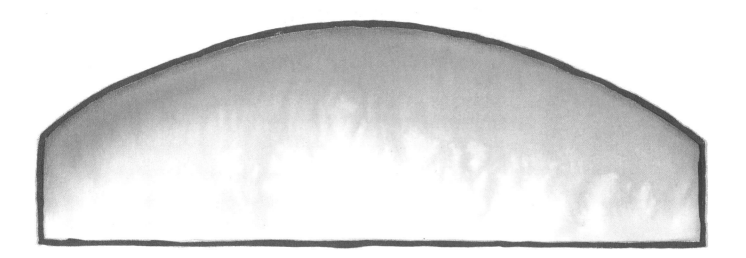

Then God divided the waters and made the arch of the sky.
And the evening and the morning were the second day.

 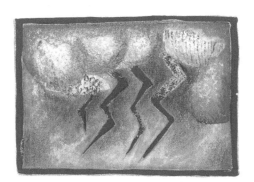 

On the third day, God gathered the waters into one place
and let the dry land appear.

God called the dry land earth and the waters
he called the sea; and he saw that it was good.

The waters rolled away and mountains and rocks
and deserts and swamps appeared. And God said, "Let
grass and trees and plants of every kind grow on the earth."

So the earth grew green and flowers bloomed and forests sprang up. The plants made seeds and spread themselves over all the earth.

And the evening and the morning were the third day.

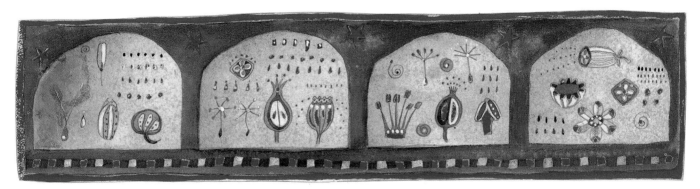

January February March April May June

Spring

Summer

On the fourth day God said, "Let there be lights in the sky to divide the day from the night, a great light called the sun to rule the day, and a lesser light called the moon to rule the night."

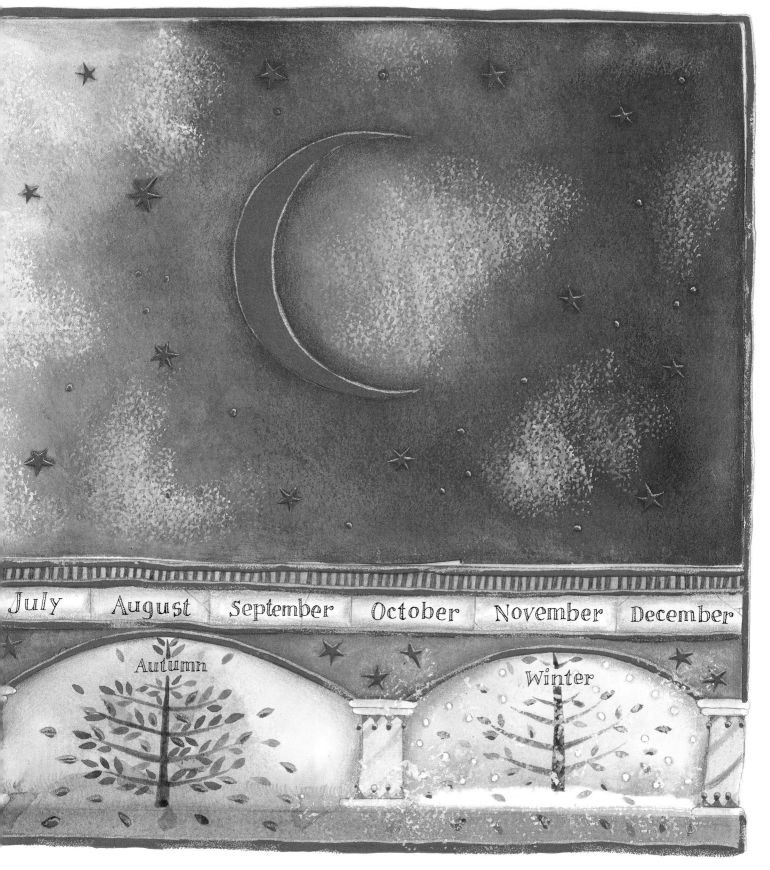

July   August   September   October   November   December

Autumn   Winter

God hung the stars in the night sky. And as day followed
night, weeks, months, years and seasons could be counted.
And the evening and the morning were the fourth day.

Now God looked at the earth and saw that it was empty,

and he said, "Let the waters bring forth living creatures."

And he filled the seas with great whales and shoals of fishes,

with dolphins, turtles, sharks, jellyfish, sealions, and sardines.

And the rivers and streams he filled with salmon and pike,
sticklebacks and minnows, otters, frogs and waterspiders.

Then God said, "Let there be birds on earth
and to fly above the earth."

And the earth was filled with the song of birds as they rose into the sky:

peacocks and flamingoes, sunbirds and turtle doves, parrots,

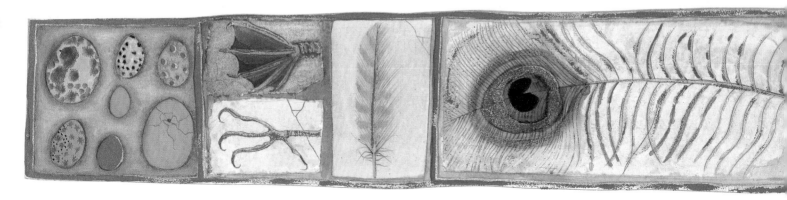

thrushes, owls, hummingbirds and nightjars.

And the evening and the morning were the fifth day.

On the sixth day God said,

"Let the earth bring forth every creature that moves,

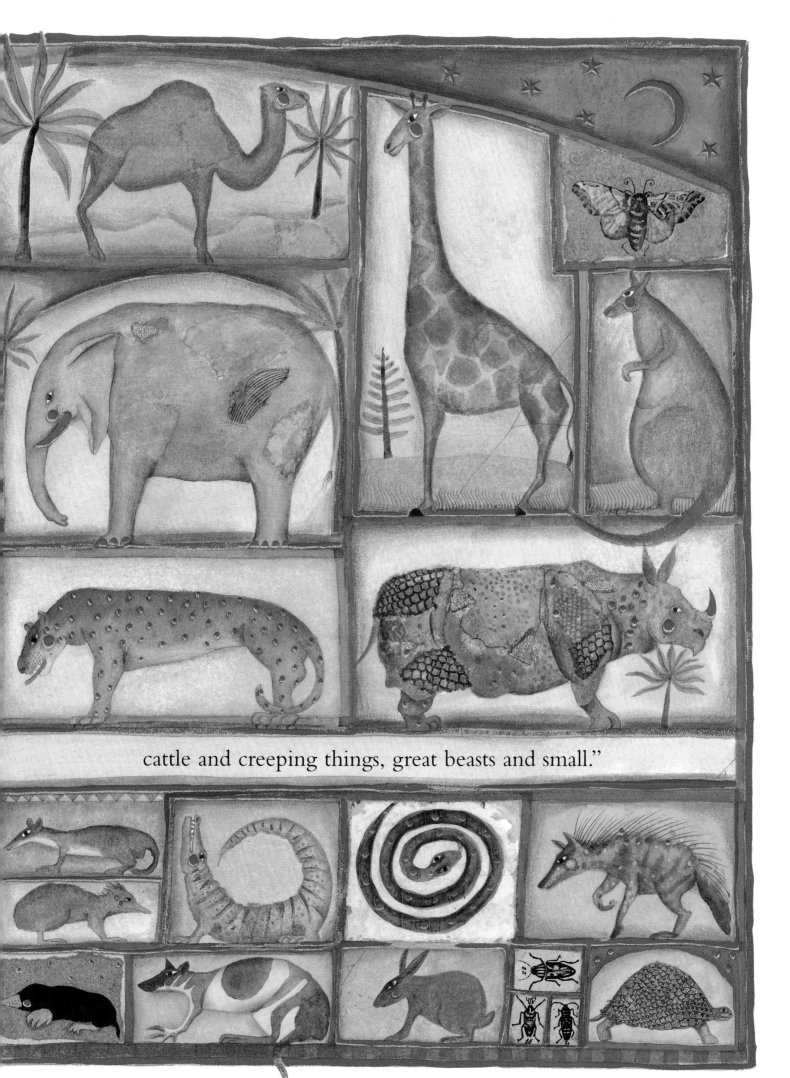

cattle and creeping things, great beasts and small."

And every creature had its own place to live in,
according to its kind, and God saw that it was good.

But God had not finished his work.

He created man and woman in his own likeness, to
take charge of the fish of the sea and the birds of the air
and the beasts of the earth and everything that grows.

Adam and Eve gave a name to every creature they saw.

And God blessed Adam and Eve and all he had created
and said, "Be fruitful and multiply and take care of the earth,
so that it may last for ever."

And the evening and the morning were the sixth day.

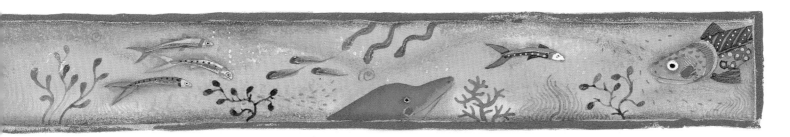

On the seventh day God finished his work,
and he was pleased with what he saw. And God
blessed the seventh day, and he rested.
And that is how the world began.

·NOAH'S·ARK·

God saw that the wickedness of man was great
in the earth, and it grieved him at his heart.

And God said, I will destroy man, and beast,
and the creeping thing, and the fowls of the air;
for it repenteth me that I have made them.

But Noah was just a man, and Noah walked
with God. And Noah begat three sons, Shem,
Ham and Japheth.

And God said unto Noah, I will cause it to
rain upon the earth forty days and forty nights;
and every thing that is in the earth shall die.
But with thee will I establish my covenant.

Make thee an ark of gopher wood. Rooms shalt thou make in the ark and shalt pitch it within and without with pitch. The length of the ark shall be three hundred cubits, the breadth fifty cubits,

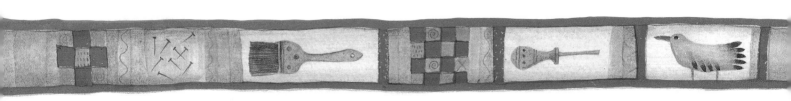

and the height of it thirty cubits.

A window shalt thou make; and the door of the ark shalt thou set in the side thereof; with lower, second, and third stories shalt thou make it.

And thou shalt come into the ark, thou, and thy sons,

and thy wife, and thy sons' wives with thee.

And of every living thing, two of every sort shalt

thou bring into the ark, the male and the female;

of fowls of the air

and of beasts, and of every thing

that creepeth upon the earth.

And take thou unto thee of all food that
is eaten; and it shall be for food for thee,
and for them. Thus did Noah, according to
all that God commanded him.

And it came to pass after seven days that
the waters of the flood were upon the earth.
The windows of heaven were opened; and
the ark went upon the face of the waters.

And all the high hills, that were under
the whole heaven, were covered.

And the mountains were covered.

Every living substance was destroyed which
was upon the ground, both man, and cattle,
and the creeping things, and the fowl of heaven.

Noah only remained alive, and they that
were with him in the ark.

And God remembered Noah, and made
a wind to pass over the earth. The rain from
heaven was restrained, and the ark rested
upon the mountains of Ararat. And the waters
decreased continually until the tops of the
mountains were seen.

And at the end of forty days Noah opened
the window of the ark and sent forth a dove, to see
if the waters were dried up from off the earth.

But she found no rest for the sole of her foot
and returned into the ark.

And Noah again sent forth the dove;
and she came in the evening and in her mouth
was an olive leaf: so Noah knew that the waters
were abated from off the earth. And at the end
of seven days Noah again sent forth the dove,
which returned not any more.

And Noah removed the covering of the ark, and looked, and behold, the face of the ground was dry.

And God spoke unto Noah, saying, I will set my bow in the cloud, and it shall be a token of a covenant between me and you and every living creature.

Go forth of the ark, thou and all thy house.
Bring forth with thee every living thing that is
with thee, both of fowl, and of cattle, and of every

creeping thing that creepeth upon the earth.
Be fruitful, and multiply, and replenish the earth.

And while the earth remaineth, seedtime
and harvest, and cold and heat, and summer
and winter, and day and night shall not cease.

·THE·STORY·OF·
·CHRISTMAS·

In the days of Herod the King, in the town of Nazareth, there lived a young girl named Mary. She was betrothed to a carpenter, whose name was Joseph.

Now the angel Gabriel was sent from God to Nazareth, to the house where Mary lived. And the angel said, "Hail, Mary! Blessed are you among women, for God has chosen you to be the mother of his Son.

You shall give birth to a baby boy, and he shall be called Jesus."

And Mary said, "Let what you have said be done."
And the angel left her.

Now it came to pass that while Mary was waiting
for the child to be born, an order went out for every

person to return to the town of his birth, so that a
count could be made of all the people in the land.

And Joseph and Mary left Nazareth together to go

to Bethlehem, where Joseph was born.

When they reached Bethlehem, Mary knew it was
time for the baby to be born. But the town was filled

with people and there was no room for them at the
inn. So the innkeeper led them to his stable.

And there Mary gave birth to her son,
and wrapped him in swaddling clothes.
She laid him in a manger, with the ox
and the ass standing by.

Now there were some shepherds in the fields
nearby, keeping watch over their flocks by night.
And the angel of the Lord appeared before them,
and the glory of the Lord shone around.

The shepherds crouched, trembling, among their

sheep but the angel said to them: "Fear not,
for I bring you tidings of great joy! For today in
Bethlehem a child is born and he is Christ the Lord.
This is a sign to you, that you will find the baby
wrapped in swaddling clothes, lying in a manger."

And a great multitude of heaven's angels appeared,
praising God and singing,

"Glory to God in the highest and peace on earth, goodwill to all men."

The shepherds left their flocks and hurried to
the stable; and when they found Mary and Joseph

and the baby lying in a manger, they knelt before him
and worshipped him.

Then they returned home, praising God
for all that they had seen, and all the people

who heard them hastened to Bethlehem
to see the holy baby for themselves.

There came also three wise men from the east,
who had seen a bright star in the skies. Bearing gifts,
they travelled far across seas and mountains, until
they reached the city of Jerusalem.

"Where is the baby who is born to be King?"
they asked. "We have seen his star in the east,
and have come to worship him."

Now King Herod was troubled when he heard of this other king, more powerful than himself. And he sent for the wise men, saying, "Go and search for the child

and return to me once you have found him,
so that I too may come and worship him."
But the King meant to do him harm.

And the star shone bright in the skies,
guiding the wise men onwards,

till it led them to Bethlehem,
and the stable where the baby lay.

And when they found the baby with Mary,
his mother, the wise men laid their gifts before him
and worshipped him on bended knee.

Then they opened up their treasures for the baby –
gold, and frankincense, and myrrh.

But being warned by God in a dream not to return
to King Herod, they departed to their own country
by another way.

And in time Joseph took Mary and the baby Jesus
home to Nazareth, and the baby grew tall and strong:
and the grace of God was upon him.

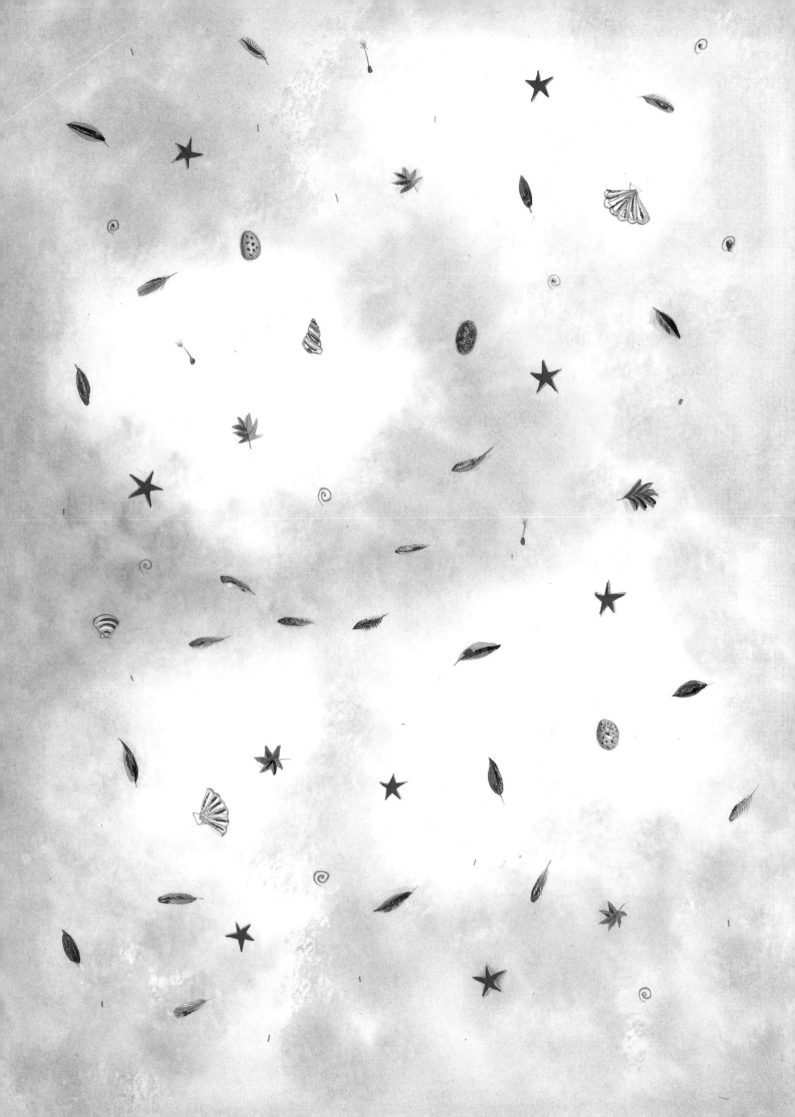